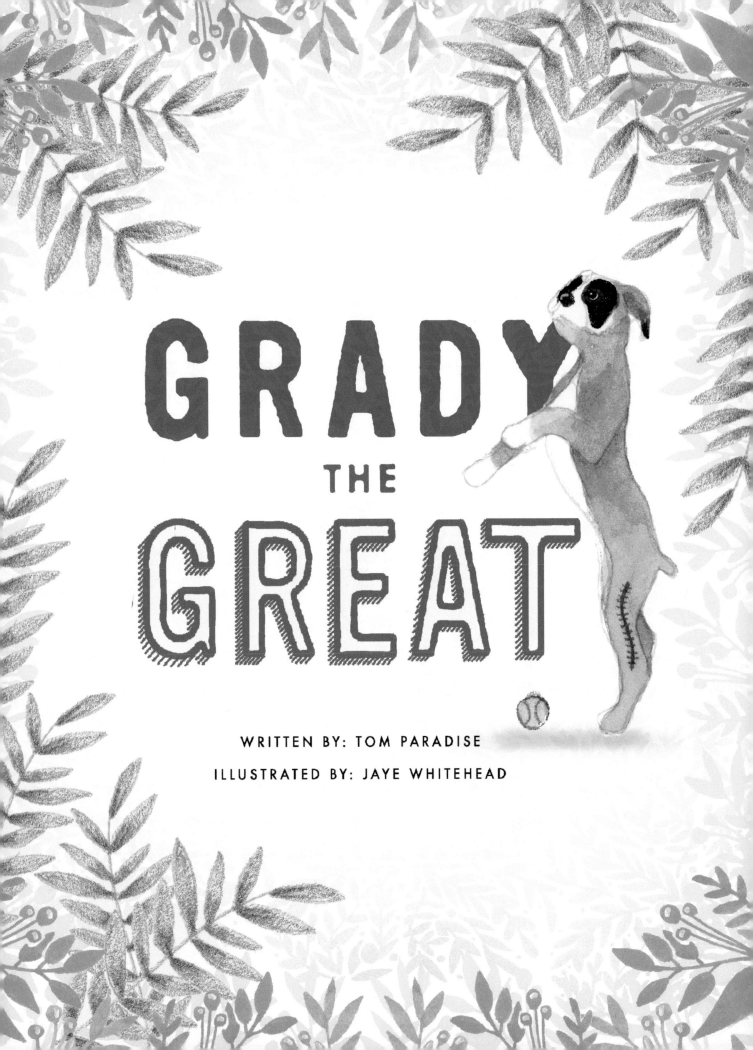

GRADY
THE
GREAT

WRITTEN BY: TOM PARADISE

ILLUSTRATED BY: JAYE WHITEHEAD

Archway Publishing books may be ordered through booksellers or by contacting:

Archway Publishing
1663 Liberty Drive
Bloomington, IN 47403
www.archwaypublishing.com
1 (888) 242-5904

ISBN: 978-1-4808-5907-4 (sc)
ISBN: 978-1-4808-5908-1 (e)

Print information available on the last page.

Archway Publishing rev. date: 05/24/2018

GRADY

THE

GREAT

Puppies, puppies, lots of puppies.

Some big, some small,

some short, some tall.

They are all so beautiful.

There are too many puppies
for us to keep.
We will give them to friends
where they will play, eat, and sleep.

Some brown, some spotted,

all with wiggly tails.

But one little boxer

had a leg that was frail.

It's not straight
and it looks rather sore.
Who wants a dog
that can only lay on the floor?

FREE PUPPY

One by one

the puppies left for a new home.

But no one seemed to want

the boxer that had a lopsided bone.

My, oh my
What should we do?
Let's call the nice people
at the boxer rescue.

The boxer team arrived

and help they gave.

They found the right vet.

The puppy was brave.

It wasn't that simple.

It could make some feel queasy.

"I have to reset the paw" said the vet.

"But it won't be easy."

I must straighten the bone
that his paw connects to.
He will be able to run.
He will be like brand new.

Leave him with me.

He will need some rest.

It's the right thing to do.

This lopsided boxer will be my guest.

My schedule is busy.
But here's what I'll do:
I'll operate on this dog,
whose healthy paws number three.
I'll do my very best
and I'll do it for free.

The surgery was a success.

The bone was repaired.

But now the puppy needs a new home

with a family that will give him good care.

It didn't take long

before a family took him home.

With two other boxers

and a big yard to roam.

His leg got stronger after the repair.
With his boxer buddies around
he was glad to be there.

But the couple with dogs
that now numbered three,
started to move apart,
started to disagree.

The couple divorced.
It was a sad day.
They agreed it would be best
to go different ways.

They each took a dog.
That's the only fair way.
But unfortunately, we must
give our boxer puppy away.

So off again to a new home.

But where would that be?

The puppy wondered, would I be alone

or would I be three?

Animal rescue was back on the job.
Many good people were waiting.
This time they found the perfect home
there could be no debating.

So when the phone rang
and they told me his story.
I headed straight for the shelter,
I was in all my glory.

From the moment I saw him

I knew it was meant to be.

The perfect name is Grady,

and his forever home is now with me.

Printed in the United States
By Bookmasters